First English edition published by Colour Library Books Ltd.
© 1984 Illustrations and text: Colour Library International Ltd.
   99 Park Avenue, New York, N.Y. 10016, U.S.A.
This edition is published by Crescent Books
Distributed by Crown Publishers, Inc.
h g f e d c b a
Colour separations by REPROCOLOR LLOVET, Barcelona, Spain.
Display and text filmsetting by ACESETTERS LTD., Richmond, Surrey, England.
Printed and bound by JISA-RIEUSSET and EUROBINDER - Barcelona (Spain)
ISBN 0 517 460 106
CRESCENT 1984

Touch of Lace

Peter Barry

CRESCENT BOOKS
NEW YORK